Dispatched

CARL THOMAS

Burning Bulb

PUBLISHING

Dispatched
By **Carl Thomas**

Burning Bulb Publishing
P.O. Box 4721
Bridgeport, WV 26330-4721
United States of America
www.BurningBulbPress.com
Book/Movie website: *www.PoliceDrama.com*

First Edition.

Paperback Edition ISBN: 978-1-948278-18-8

Printed in the United States of America

"I thought I was being arrested by a normal Police Officer. Not so! Carl Thomas is different.

"His concern for me was genuine, and carried no agenda. He loved me without condition when I was unlovable. He TRULY cared, both in word and deed and it opened my eyes to Christ's unconditional love! He leads by example. Truly a great man!"

— Bill Donahue

"It has been my pleasure and honor to know and minister with Carl Thomas for over 25 years in prison ministry outreach. I call him "faithful" in his commitment to the Gospel of Jesus Christ – to what many consider the worthless of our society. The inmates simply love this former retired police officer. God has well prepared this man in all aspects for this good work! A former Special Forces/Green beret, Vietnam Veteran, he has learned and applies the disciplines of a true soldier, the compassion towards broken humanity with a "new hope" for their lives and days ahead. My wife Susan and I love and respect him **so much**! A friend, a brother, a servant of the Lord's choosing.

"May all who see this wonderful man's life's testimony in movie and/or book have a blessed "Barnabas" experience in their lives and ministry in building God's Kingdom!"

— Wayne R. Baldwin, Pastor
Crossroads Christian Ministry
Oakham, MA 01068

"I have been friends with Carl Thomas since 1970. Carl and I both worked on a local police department for approximately 25 years. Carl was a dedicated police officer, but struggled with temper and violence issues. He had a temper and would often get involved in physical altercations with suspects, criminals and occasionally other people. Carl had served several tours of duty during the Vietnam War and definitely carried the mental scars resulting from the trauma.

"One afternoon in the late 1980's, Carl, my wife, another couple and I attended a healing service in Worcester, Mass. conducted by Father DiOrio. At the time, my wife suffered from Multiple Sclerosis and was suffering from blurry vision. Her doctor at the time told her that it would be something she had to live with. As Father DiOrio was praying over us, her vision cleared and to this day, her vision is clear. It was obvious that much more was happening. The five of us left the healing service with healed souls. We all became active in our various churches and attended bible studies and began a new relationship with the Lord.

"The effects of the Holy Spirit were even more noticeable with Carl. Carl immediately became more compassionate and concerned with others. He no longer resorted to physical violence as he had in the past It was clear that his heart was opened by Jesus.

"Carl began sharing the Word of God with anyone who was suffering both mentally or physically.

"He prayed with those who were troubled. Shortly thereafter, he started a prison ministry which continues today. I have personally known several people who turned their lives over to Jesus as a result of their relationship with Carl.

"I am proud to be a friend and brother with this outstanding man."

— Greg Deschamps

FOREWORD 1

I joined the Windsor Police Department in 1983, at the age of 21. Many of the officers on the force were Vietnam veterans and were products of 1960-70 era policing. Their approach to law enforcement was heavy handed and I was told that nobody had a heavier hand than Officer Carl Thomas, or "CT" as he was called. I had heard stories about how "CT" would respond to domestic disputes, and whenever he learned that a man had struck a woman, he would challenge the man to a fight, challenging his toughness. The criminal element in town feared "CT" and openly told me about how Officer Thomas would beat them up if he caught them out of line.

I never witnessed any of these traits, because right around 1983, "CT - found God". Carl turned his life over to Christ, and with that he was a changed man. Many of his peers were skeptical, but in the years that followed from his being born again to his retirement, Carl was a caring and compassionate man. Make no mistake, he was still the toughest man I have ever had the privilege to serve with, but he never displayed the anger and aggression that I had been told existed. Instead, he was a mentor and an inspiration to me as a police officer and as a man.

—Captain Tom LePore
Windsor Police Department

FOREWORD 2

I first met Carl Thomas in 1977. My father owned a family owned restaurant (Bart's) in Windsor CT. My father knew all the local law enforcement officers as they visited the restaurant daily. This was soon after my brother died in a drowning accident, he was a shining star in our family's life. I became interested in martial arts and my father knew Carl Thomas, a police officer of Windsor who was Green Beret Vietnam Veteran and martial art expert. My Father was friendly with Carl and asked him if he would be interested in giving me karate lessons. Carl new of my recent loss and was more than willing to train me.

I remember to this day, my father driving me to Carl's home in Enfield CT. My father would drop me off and pick me up a few hours or Carl would drive me home. The friendship grew immediately. Carl was not only a martial art expert, but I learned that he was kind person who loved sharing with others. I was also taking traditional martial arts lessons at the time, but Carl's teaching methods were completely different. He said if you want how to learn to fight you have to learn to take the punishment. Along with training with people twice my age and size, I recall to this day Carl would bring me on long runs chanting green beret chants and themes that I can still sing for you today.

Carl became not only a martial art instructor but my mentor and friend. I admired him and I strived to be like him. Think about it, I was a young teenager being personally trained by a Green Beret.

Our two families very quickly became close friends. I would train with Carl and stay over weekends. I would become the family babysitter for the girls, attending picnics with the Thomas family and also trained with Carl's Brother, who was also a Green Beret.

Carl's was a police officer in my Town. I started to ride with him on a regular basis. Throughout my teenage years I would train with

Carl on weekends and ride with him while he was on duty. This is how my career direction in life was developed.

I also saw and learned what violence can be as a police officer on the street. There were several times I started to put my skills to the test on the street. When Carl heard of this there was a quick and personal visit from him to my house. He would not accept me becoming a street fighter and trust me as tough as you think you are when you are confronted by Carl Thomas you realize what you're up against. He was truly an older brother figure to me.

As I rode with Carl on many of many occasions , I witnessed many police engagements, I saw how Carl could be dark and very violent. But yet the same person would spend hours consoling someone who just lost a family member.

I knew as young teenager that I wanted to be a police officer like my mentor Carl Thomas. My whole focus was to become a police officer at which Carl helped me and provided me tutelage on how to obtain that goal.

I became a police officer in 1980 a year out of high school. As a full time police officer I saw how my friend Carl was heading towards a downward spiral. Carl had anger issues that I did not identify or understand at the time. I knew he was in Vietnam but did not understand how this effected his life. I also learned about Carl's upbringing being so different than mine.

I did see how unless he changed his career would heading towards trouble.

I remember when Carl found God. He was elated and wanted to share with everyone. I was very resistant as I had no interest and no belief. This was soon after my brother died in a pool accident and my other brother suffered traumatic brain injury by a doctor's misdiagnosis. In my brain what type of God would do this to my parents. Although I respected my mentor, I did not follow his path. He was patient with me and never pushed his spiritual revelations on me. My sister once described him in the best way. She said, Carl won the lottery and it changed his life so much for the better that he wanted to share and give it to those he loved. Carl's finding God completely changed him. It minimized his anger, he understood his word, he became forgiving and changed his life. There is no doubt in my mind that it changed Carl's life for the good and Carl dedicated the rest of his life giving to others. He truly did win the lottery and shared his spiritual knowledge and love with as many others as he could, including the very same people he put in prison. Carl was in fact what he preached, forgive those who trespass against us…and those he loves.

Carl changed and influenced my life and will always be a part of who I am today. I believe God was always within him but comes to all of us in different ways and in different times. Carl was always giving sharing in and caring person who has always given to others.

—Lt. Kevin F. Dillon (Ret)

FOREWORD 3

I first met Carl when he attended a Strong Enough Men's Retreat. A year or two later, Carl was invited back to be on the Strong Enough Team, which was preparing for its biannual retreat.

While serving with Carl on this team is when I had the opportunity to hear of his life story. Carl is a gentleman of around 70 years old—a very polite and caring man. He is a man who has committed all he is to his Lord Jesus Christ.

What intrigued me so much about Carl was when he shared with me the man he used to be. Carl was a Green Beret Vietnam Veteran and a career Windsor Police Officer. He also shared that through all those years, he had some serious anger issues.

Even more intriguing was hearing of the conversion Carl had midway through his law enforcement career. It was at that time he came face to face with God, our creator, who poured his love into Carl. This miraculous encounter transformed this angry man into a gentleman and the man of God you see today.

As I listened to his story unfold, I could see that there was a good person deep inside. Years of hurt and built up anger overshadowed who God created this man to be.

Carl always said, "Only God, could do this healing work within a human being."

As I listened to his stories, vivid scenes were flooding my mind of what Carl's life was like before and after Christ.

Just earlier that year, before meeting Carl, God had connected me with both a Christian Book Publisher and a Christian Movie Producer.

After a conversation with both of these organizations concerning Carl's story, I then approached Carl and said, "I'm just putting this out there, and you can discern if this is from the Lord or not. I feel like your life's story should be published as a book."

I then told Carl, "Besides writing a book, I have also made connections with a movie producer. We believe that this should head into the direction of both a book and movie."

It took steps of faith on many levels:

- from Carl sharing his story,
- to Carl and I venturing into a book and movie project (something we had never done before, nor ever dreamed we would be involved in),
- to publishers and producers saying, "Yes, this is something worth pursuing.",
- to people stepping up with financial backing,
- to people being willing to help spread this project throughout the country.

I see God's involvement in moving this project forward so very quickly. It was much more significant than we could ever imagined. As we have put our faith in Him, He has steadily unfolded His plan of reaching hurting people in this world.

"Only God!"

As for the Strong Enough Men's Retreat, it was first started in 2012 by Bob Wilson and a small group of men whose desire was to help strengthen other men's faith in Jesus Christ. God had laid it on the hearts of this men's group to share the real struggles that men deal with daily and to take to heart the scripture in 2 Corinthians 12:9-10 that concludes with, "For when I am weak, then I am strong."

Dispatched was a takeaway from one of the Strong Enough retreats. It is the desire of the Strong Enough Ministry to see this retreat expand to other churches across the nation. If you would like to get information concerning this retreat, please contact us at info@strongenoughretreat.org.

—Bob Wilson
Founder of the Strong Enough Men's Ministry

ACKNOWLEDGEMENTS

My story is dedicated to my Lord and Savior Jesus Christ. If not for Him, there would be no book. I would have no story to tell! To Him be all the glory!

The many times I have fallen, and failed, God's grace was always there to help me through the dark times; always there to keep me running the race. As bad as it was at times, my wife Vicki was always there praying for me, and encouraging me to keep on keeping on.

Also, I would like to acknowledge our children, Melissa, Stephanie, Missy, and Mark, as well as their spouses, Alex, Joe, Shawn, Sandy, and also my nephew Joshua. Then of course all my grandchildren, Taylor, Mia, Isaiah, Justin, Oliver, Noah, Isaac and my great grandchild Paxton.

A special thanks to my sister Elizabeth for her help in putting my story together. Thanks to my brothers, Bruce and Chris, for keeping me in line along the way. Thank you, mom, dad, and my brother Joe, for your love and for always believing in me. One day we will meet again in Heaven.

A special thank you to Bob Wilson, founder and director of "Strong Enough Men's Ministries". When Bob heard me give my story at the men's retreat, November 2018, he caught the vision that this story could reach lost and hurting souls.

INTRODUCTION
Making a deal with God

I don't normally make deals with God. However, this one particular Saturday afternoon, while on patrol, I did.

"Base to all units, base to all units, a high-speed chase coming through town, with several towns pursuing a white Corvette, driven by an escapee from the a Midwestern correctional facility. Chase is now northbound on Rt. 75."

Hey that's my area! Off I went toward Rt. 75, in hopes of joining the chase. By the time I got to the area, the chase had already left Windsor, heading west on Rt. 20, toward the Granby area. "One twelve (that's me) to base, permission to leave town to assist in the pursuit."

"Go ahead One Twelve."

To myself I shouted, *YES!*

The man that we were pursuing was an escapee named Kenny. He was doing time for tying up a senior citizen and raping her. The reason he was in our immediate area is because he had family living in Granby. When it was discovered that it was Kenny we were pursuing, it became imperative that we catch him and take him in.

While heading west on Rt. 20 I remember praying, "Lord let me be the one to catch this guy. If You let me be the one to capture him Lord, I will witness to him. In Jesus name, amen!"

When I got to Granby, I turned south on Rt. 202 and 10. I really had no idea where the chase was at this time. As I'm heading south, I can see up ahead, what appeared to be two plainclothes cops pursuing a man on foot, running across the highway.

That's got to be Kenny they're chasing!

I sped up to the area where I saw the foot pursuit. When I parked my car and jumped out, I started running toward a wooded area. I only caught a glimpse of the last man running through the woods. At least I knew I was running in the right direction.

When I finally made it to the other side of the woods, I came out onto a large clearing. As I looked across the field, two men were just standing there doing nothing. I ran up to their location.

Out of breath I asked, "Where did he go?"

They pointed toward the Farmington River. "He swam across the river. He's long gone."

When I looked up in the air and saw the helicopter that was following Kenny go farther and farther away from the river, I knew right then and there I wasn't going to be the one capturing this guy. I turned and started walking back toward my cruiser. I didn't get too far, when I heard the whirring of the helicopter getting louder and louder. I looked up, and sure enough the chopper was coming back toward the river.

Oh my gosh! That must mean that Kenny turned around and is heading back toward the river as well!

I immediately started running in a northerly direction toward the river to align myself with the chopper. When I got to the top of the river bank and looked down, there was Kenny, coming out of the water right in front of me!

"Freeze! Don't move!" I shouted, as I aimed my service revolver at him. He looked at me and started walking up the river bank toward me. It was obvious he wasn't going to stop. It was also quite obvious he didn't have a gun or any other type of weapon on his body. There was no way I could shoot him. I then holstered my weapon and took out my pepper spray.

When he was only a few feet from me, still walking toward me, I sprayed him in the face, mostly in the eyes. He turned around screaming and then he ran back into the river. I pursued him into the river, as he was trying to purge his eyes with the water.

I was able to grab him from behind, drag him out of the water, and throw him down on the ground. As I sat on his back, I wrestled one hand behind his back and cuffed it. When I tried cuffing the other hand, he resisted.

At about the same time, a Suffield cop ran down the river bank to assist me. As we were struggling with Kenny to cuff the other hand, a State Police canine jumped on the pile and started taking a bite out of my left knee!

No sooner did he start taking a bite, his trainer yelled: "Not him! Him!" The well-trained canine immediately let go of me and started biting on Kenny.

Kenny was placed under arrest and taken into State Police custody.

All the way back to my cruiser I praised God, and thank Him for letting me be the one to catch Kenny! "Jesus, you are so awesome! Thank You, thank You, thank You!"

Then, as a friendly reminder, God reminded me: "Don't forget Carl, you made a deal with Me. I kept up My end of it."

"Yes Lord, I will keep up mine as well."

I never did get any recognition for the capture of Kenny. The state police took all the credit, adding they were assisted by town police in taking Kenny into custody. It really didn't matter to me. I knew and God knew, and that's all that really mattered.

Actually, what truly mattered was what happened the following Monday morning.

That morning Kenny was being transported from the State Police barracks in Hartford to the court house in Enfield. When I reported for duty that Monday morning, I went straight to the Chief's office.

Chief Searles was not only my Chief, he was also my brother in Christ. So, when I explained to him the deal I made with Jesus, he gave me permission to go to Enfield and witness to Kenny.

When I got to Enfield, I met with the Head Sheriff, who happened to be a personal friend of mine. Joe broke protocol and let me in a small room with Kenny.

When Kenny walked in the room and saw me, he immediately started shouting at me: "YOU'RE THE F**KING A**HOLE that sprayed me with that pepper spray!"

"Yes, Kenny I am, but I'm not here to hurt you now. I'm here to tell you something that you need to hear. Please hear me out."

Miraculously, Kenny calmed right down. I told him that God sent me to tell him that He loves him, and that Jesus died for every sin, for every crime that he has ever committed.

If he would confess to Him and turn away from the life that he has been living and turn his life over to Jesus, he would be forgiven, and be made into a new man, and be given a new life.

Under the anointing of the Holy Spirit I saw Kenny's eyes well up with tears, tears streaming down his face as the room filled up with God's Presence.

"Would you like to pray with me Kenny? Jesus is knocking onto the door of your heart. If you ask Him to come in, He will, and be with you for the whole rest of your life. As you make the choice to follow Him, He will never leave you nor forsake you."

Right there in that room we joined hands and we prayed, while all the angels in Heaven were rejoicing!

The word of God says that, "He sent His only begotten Son to die for the whole world, every man, woman, and child so that whoever believes in Him should not perish but have everlasting life."

Notice in the Word of God there are no exceptions! We are all sinners. Just like Jesus came out to save me in Worcester, Massachusetts, He came out to save Kenny that day in Enfield, Connecticut.

PROLOGUE

My story is not about me, but rather it is about God and His amazing grace. My prayer is that you, the reader, will see throughout this book, God's incredible love displayed for us, His creation. God's love is on display for every man, woman, and child, if we would only take the time to see it.

I pray that my personal story would reveal to you that our God lives. He is here with us, moving in our midst, reaching out to every broken heart and every lost soul. He is here to shine His light into our darkness, in order to make a way where there seems to be no way. He is a miracle worker—that is who He is.

My story reveals that there are no exceptions to God's love. Jesus died for the whole world, for every sin, every crime ever committed by man. It is His heart's desire to take us out of our present darkness and bring us into His glorious light.

Not only does God want to save us, He also wants to transform us into new beings. You have no idea what God can—and will do—in you and through you once you surrender your life into His hands.

We serve a mighty God. I pray that you, the reader, will come to believe that there is no other name above the name of Jesus Christ. Jesus wants to save, deliver, and restore us with His redeeming love, and His transforming power.

I pray that this book shows, without exception, that Jesus Christ is the Way, the Truth, and the Life. Be blessed.

THE GOOD OLD DAYS

I am a post WWII baby. My dad returned home from fighting after three years in the South Pacific. When he returned from the war, he met my mom and married her in June of 1946. I was born nine months later in February 1947, into a very Italian patriarchal home.

Italian? How can the name Thomas be Italian? When my Grandfather came over to the United States from Italy to become an American citizen, he Americanized his last name from DiTomaso to Thomas. My mother's maiden name was Cascone. Her parents came over from Sicily.

I'm the oldest of four siblings. My brother, Bruce, arrived two years after me, then Joey, Elizabeth, and finally Christopher, eighteen years later, when I was getting ready to graduate high school.

For the first three years of my life, we lived in a three-story tenement building in the north end of Hartford, CT. Our time living in Hartford ended abruptly when I decided to walk across North Main Street, unattended. Right then and there, my dad and mom decided it was time to move to the suburbs.

As I look back on it now, the only reason why I was able to cross that busy road without getting hurt or killed was because my Heavenly Father already had a plan for my life, and it didn't involve me getting hit by a car. For the next thirteen years, I lived, played, and grew up in East Hartford, CT.

Our home was right next door to a town park. The properties were divided by an old broken-down fence. The park consisted of swings and slides and a merry-go-round, along with a public pool. This neighborhood was full of post-World War II babies, all of us playing until the sun went down and the street lights came on. It was certainly a great time to be a kid.

On the other side of the park was an elementary school. Even at age seventy-two, I still remember the names of every teacher I ever had. I have so many fond memories of the neighborhood I grew up in.

As for my dad, he was a hard-working mechanic. There was nothing about a car he couldn't fix. When he'd come home at the end of the day, my mom made sure supper was ready, along with us kids lined up at the top of the stairs waiting to greet him.

He was demanding! His orders were loud and clear!

My mom was very subservient. "Mother! Get me my glasses! Mother! Make me a sandwich! Mother! Where are my shoes?" He would yell, then go back to working on his crossword puzzle.

Or he'd shout, "Son, change the channel. Son, get me an ashtray. Son, where's my bowling ball?"

No one ever dared to talk back. If anyone even thought of defying him, there were consequences. I never saw my dad hit my mom or my sister, but for me and my brothers, it was totally different!

Before I go any further, I just want to make clear that my mom and dad were very loving parents, and so proud of each of us. My dad was always bragging about his kids, and it got to the point where people got tired of listening to him. My parents were good and generous to so many people. We were the only ones in the family who lived in the suburbs. We not only had a house; we also had a television. All my aunts, uncles, and cousins lived in apartments in the city. Every weekend, they would all come to visit. My mom would lay out a spread, along with plain, good old-fashioned Italian hospitality. Everybody loved coming to the Thomas'. With a park and swimming pool next door, it was an oasis from the big city.

***

I remember good times with my dad as well—having a catch in the backyard, going to Soundview Beach almost every weekend in the summer, and going to Yankee Stadium to see Mantle and Maris. They were the good old days for sure.

The year I turned nine, I tried out for Little League baseball. Due to my dad's coaching, I got picked to play on the JAYCEES team. My dad came to every game to see me play, even if it meant seeing me warm the bench. It didn't matter if I played or not, my dad loved me and was proud of me.

Despite what I'm going to say next, I loved him too.

Like I said earlier, my dad spent three years fighting a war in the South Pacific. The extreme atrocities and horrors he encountered wounded my dad more so than any physical wound he could have received. It's only in putting my story together that I have come to realize that as a result of the war, my dad suffered from Post-Traumatic Stress Disorder, better known as PTSD.

My dad could be the nicest guy in the world, but he was a walking time bomb. At the flick of a switch, he would suddenly become this monster! He could be emotionally and physically abusive over a slight infraction of his way of doing things. If we were noncompliant, my brothers and I would suffer terrible beatings, kicks, body punches, or hard slaps across the face. This was his way of disciplining us.

Other times he would just yell out my name, "Carl! Get over here!" Just hearing his voice caused utter fear! As scared as I was, though, I came. If I tried to run or hide, like I sometimes did, he would find me, and the beating would be worse.

When I came and stood at attention in front of him, he'd say, "Don't move! Don't even blink!" Then I'd get an open hand across the face. If I moved or cried, another hard whack would follow.

There were times I went to school with my father's handprint across the left side of my face. I wanted to fight back, but there was no way I could. I wasn't big enough or strong enough, nor was I foolish enough to fight back.

I do remember one time, though, when my dad was disciplining Bruce with punches, kicks, and slaps. I wanted to protect my brother, so I got between them, dragging Bruce out of the house, taking the blows as we escaped.

Worse than the abuse, I was becoming like my dad.

I had a heart of gold. Even as a kid I would do anything for you. I was always sticking up for the underdog. If someone started pushing on someone smaller, or younger, or if someone tried to hurt me, or say mean things to me, I became easily provoked and very combative.

In 1965, I graduated from high school. It was also in 1965, that I received my last beating from my father. I hated the way he treated my mom. She was more servant than wife. I wasn't a little guy anymore. I was captain of the school's wrestling team and I could throw a discus 145 feet. I wasn't afraid of him anymore.

I stood in the middle of the living room floor one day shouting down at him as he sat in his chair. "I will never treat the woman I marry the way you treat my mother!"

Like a volcano erupting, he exploded on me. Since I was much bigger and stronger now, I stood fast and wouldn't let him move me.

At the same time, I began taunting him. "Is that all you got, is that all you got? Go ahead. Hit me! You can't hurt me!"

Finally, he stopped, and the beatings stopped. They stopped for me, but not for my brothers Bruce and Joey.

*Carl with his brothers and sister. From left to right
Carl, Bruce, Joey, Elizabeth, and Chris.*

ARMY SPECIAL FORCES (GREEN BERET)

After graduating from high school in 1965, I went to Central Connecticut State Teachers College, with all intention of becoming a school teacher. It took only six months for me to realize that college just wasn't my thing. I dropped out, and walked away from furthering my education.

A few months later, I got a letter from Uncle Sam wanting to draft me into the military. Since the Vietnam War was going on at that time, I refused to be drafted. That meant they could do anything they wanted with me. They could send me anywhere they chose to send me, so, I chose to enlist into the United States Army.

At that time, the song *The Ballad of the Green Berets* was very popular. "Fighting soldiers from the sky. Fearless men who jump and die. Men who mean just what they say. The brave men, of the Green Beret." After hearing the words to this song, I knew that if I was going to Vietnam, these were the men I wanted to go to war with.

After my first year of Infantry Training, I went for three weeks to Ft. Benning, Georgia, for Jump School. You needed to be jump-qualified before becoming a Green Beret. After making my fifth parachute jump, I had silver wings pinned on my chest.

From Ft. Benning I went to Ft. Bragg, NC, to receive the most intense jungle and guerilla warfare training known to man. I remember the survival tactics, evasion, resistance and escape tactics we were trained in. If we were ever captured and taken prisoner during our war games, we would be taken to a mock POW camp. Our captors would try to break us, get us to divulge classified information. I remember the stretching machine. If you got captured you would be put on this contraption and stretched until you couldn't be stretched anymore and then a little bit more!

Our training was during the winter months. Prisoners would also be thrown into frigid waters. Before hypothermia would set in you would be taken out of the water and sat down by a fire. Just when you started warming up, you got thrown back into the water. This would happen again and again and again! Let's put it this way: a lot of Special Forces trainees dropped out of the program due to this portion of training.

We were also trained in self-defense, weaponry, demolitions, communications, as well as medical training. When the training was finally over, out of the 300 men that started, only 75 men stood in formation to win the honor of wearing the Green Beret. I was one of the 75! .

After my training was complete, instead of going to Vietnam, I was assigned to the 1st Special Forces Group. I was to spend the next eighteen months in Okinawa. My mission was to give refresher training courses in jungle warfare to soldiers on their way to Vietnam.

Shortly after my eighteen months were up, I was assigned to the Central Highlands of Vietnam. It turned out that my year in Vietnam, from 1971-1972, greatly compounded my anger issues. That year was a living hell. If it wasn't for the intense training I received in the states, I know I wouldn't be here writing this book.

Seeing my buddy, Sgt. Kevin D. Grogan, shot in the neck, and dying in my arms in the middle of a firefight, is still a living nightmare for me. Halfway through my tour in Vietnam, I put in for R & R for two weeks. R & R stands for rest and recuperation away from the war zone.

Most of the guys went to Thailand or Australia. Not me. Put me on a plane! I'm going home! I was so glad to be going home, even if it was only for two weeks.

Toward the end of my R & R, I was having second thoughts about returning for another six months in Nam. I remember my dad telling me he had connections and that he could work it out so that I wouldn't have to return. Then he said, "Son, if you don't go back and finish what you started, it's your face you will have to look at in the mirror for the rest of your life."

I knew what my dad was saying. As hard as it was for me and my family, I returned to Vietnam to finish out the rest of my tour.

Once my tour of duty was up, I came back to the states and left the military. As a result of my upbringing, and fighting in a war, I became just like my father! Even though PTSD was still not recognized at the time, I suffered from it as well.

Dedicated to
Sgt. Kevin D. Grogan
US Army,
5th Special Forces Group

DISPATCHED BY MAN

Shortly after leaving the military, I was in search of a job. I had no idea what I was going to do, or even what I wanted to do. My brother Bruce, now an East Hartford police officer, approached me one day and said, "Hey, why not be a cop?" The thought of being a police officer started to appeal to me. It offered both good pay and benefits, which happened to include a retirement program after twenty-five years of service.

Besides, at this point, I had a girlfriend I wanted to marry. I needed a job. I started filling out applications to several local police departments, including the Connecticut State Police. The Windsor Police Department was the first department to call me and ask me to come in for an interview.

The first question the oral board asked me was, "Why do you want to be a police officer?"

My answer was, "I want to help people."

The next question was, "What kind of background do you have?"

My answer to that was, "I just served four years and eight months in the United States Army, doing one year in Vietnam with Army Special Forces."

"Great! You're just the kind of guy we're looking for. You're hired!"

In May of 1973, I graduated from the police academy and became a police officer for the town of Windsor, CT. In September 1973, my first wife and I walked down the aisle.

It didn't take long before my anger issues were put on full display. It was actually with another cop who got in my face and told me, "You do what I tell you to do!"

Just because I was a rookie cop, he thought he could order me around. I was so enraged, I shouted back: "Excuse me! I don't think so!"

Before this officer had time to think, he was flat on his back, with me bending over him yelling, "Don't even think about getting up!"

I didn't get in trouble for that incident. Instead, I got respect from the other officers, including my supervisors. I wasn't somebody you could push around and get away with it. I really liked my job as a police officer. Every day was different. You never knew what kind of call you were going to get next. Like Forest Gump would say, "Life is like a box of chocolates. You never know what you're going to get."

To mention a few, I was dispatched to motor vehicle accidents, sick calls, burglaries, domestic disturbances, robbery in progress, breach of peace, and yes, even a cat in a tree, or a squirrel running around in someone's house. Even though there was downtime, my job was far from boring, and I was loving it. I had opportunities galore to help others, serve others, and yes, arrest the bad guys, the law breakers, and lock them up so they received the justice they deserved.

For the most part, I had a good heart. Just like my mom and dad, I would go the extra mile for someone, especially with troubled or hurting youth. As a police officer, I had the opportunity to take a young teenage boy under my wing and do everything I possibly could to steer him in the right direction.

One such boy was Kevin. Kevin was only fourteen years old when he lost his sixteen-year-old brother, Bobby, in a pool accident. At that time, I had a reputation of knowing the martial arts. Kevin's dad, a business man in town, asked me one day if I would take the time to teach his son karate.

My immediate response was, "Sure, Bob. I'd love to!"

Kevin and I immediately bonded. Not only did I become Kevin's teacher and mentor, but most of all, I became his friend.

Years later, Kevin, at the very young age of nineteen years old, got hired by the Wethersfield Police Department. Twenty-five years later he finished out his police career as a Lieutenant. Presently, he travels all over the U.S., and also into other countries, teaching police combat techniques to all the different police departments and security companies as well.

COURANT PHOTO BY JUDY GRIESEDIECK

Windsor Patrolman Carl J. Thomas shows Kevin Dillon, 17, one of the many reports police officers fill out during their patrol shift. Dillon, during the past few years, has spent several nights on patrol with Thomas. He is one of more than 30 youths to be befriended by this officer.

Windsor Patrolman Is Friend to Youth

By VIVIAN B. MARTIN

WINDSOR — Carl J. Thomas hasn't been trained in counseling or any similar field, but he's the person a few local professionals look for when they need someone to work with troubled youths.

Thomas, 32, has run what one junior high school principal describes as his own "self-styled Big Brother" program during most of the six-and-a-half years he's been a Windsor patrolman. He has taken more than 30 youths on individual outings, driven them around with him in the police cruiser, or taken them home to special dinners prepared by his wife, Maryanne. Also, Thomas has spent time working out with youths or teaching them karate, an art in which he earned a black belt while serving in the army in Okinawa.

Thomas' friends are delinquent youths, pre-delinquent youths, and, in many cases, youths who are temporarily lost. "Carl," Lt. John Riccio explains, "works with the kids everybody else has given up on." People many times have told him the youths he's working with are "rotten kids", but Thomas persists.

"I'm not saying it's the right way, but it's my way," Thomas says and then speaks of a longtime desire to help others, especially youths.

He wants them to respect the law and respect themselves. He says he also wants them to know that police officers can be their friends.

"I'm not out there to change people. I'm out there to help. Just give me a chance and I'll show you," he says. When Thomas has been given the chance, he's shown them.

Five years ago when the basketball hoop at the Hayden Station firehouse was taken down because of the vandalism done by area youths, Thomas got the youths to understand the reasons behind the move and then helped them launch a successful petition drive to get the hoop back.

Kevin Dillon, 17, has decided to pursue a career in law enforcement because of his involvement with Thomas. Dillon wasn't a delinquent; he just needed a friend at the time. His father says he's pleased with his son's relationship with Thomas.

Kids looking for help "aren't hard to find when you're a cop," Thomas says.

Locally, the Juvenile Review Board has referred cases to Thomas. Board members the Rev. Lawrence R. Bock of St. Gabriel's Church and James Snyder, vice principal of Leland P. Wilson Junior High, both also speak of the respect local youths have for Thomas.

Eugene Marchand, East Hartford youth services director and a former counselor in Windsor, says Thomas sought the review board's most challenging cases. He says Thomas volunteered for difficult cases in the local Big Friend program.

Marchand says this helped teach youths that "police officers can be human and caring. It was rather odd and startling (to youths) that some would be willing to put in time like that. It had a humanizing effect," he says.

Thomas' efforts are generally respected within the department. Patrolman Gregory Deschamps describes Thomas as "more sensitive in some ways, but also hard when its needed."

Sgt. Robert A. Nevins says Thomas' efforts are unusual because it is usually the rookie "that wants to help everybody."

But Thomas holds no illusions. Some people can't be helped, he says, though he believes that if people "let it come from your heart instead of your head" many of the people on his beat can be.

SHORT FUSED

Then there was the police officer, Carl Thomas, who wasn't so nice. So many times, in the streets, or responding to a domestic disturbance, or going to break up a fight, or shut down a loud party somewhere, there was always somebody getting in my face, challenging me, putting their hands on me, looking at me the wrong way. There were a few times that some people even spat in my face.

The fuse in me was short, very short. In a matter of seconds, I would explode on these offenders by throwing them down to the ground and wailing on them until they begged me to stop. I distinctly remember one guy saying to me, "I know where you live."

Before he could get the last word out of his mouth, he was on the ground with me on top of him, knocking him senseless. Finally, other officers dragged me off of him. He never did come to my home.

Then there were the guys I would arrest for fighting, resisting arrest, being drunk and disorderly. When you placed someone under arrest, you always cuffed them with their hands behind their back, and you placed them in the back seat of your cruiser.

There were times while in route to the police station, prisoners would often start yelling, "Hey Pig! You're nothing but a f**king punk!!!! If you didn't have that badge and that gun on, I'd kick your f**king a**!"

As we're driving to the station, instead of turning into the driveway with my prisoner, I continued driving past the PD.

"Hey! Where are you going? You just passed the police station! Where're you taking me?"

"Don't you worry about it. We'll be there in just another minute," I replied.

About a mile from the station was a warehouse. On the back side of the warehouse was nothing but woods. I drove my cruiser around to the back side of the building and parked it. I got out of my car and opened the trunk. I then took off my police shirt with the badge pinned to it and I placed it in the trunk. I then took off my gun belt and placed that in the trunk as well.

I could hear my prisoner screaming through the back window, "What are you doing? What are you doing!?"

I opened the back door, and I got in his face, "I don't have my badge or my gun on, we're going to find out who the real f**king punk is."

I explained to him that if he could beat me, not to worry, he wouldn't be charged with assaulting a police officer. If I beat him, I'll just say he resisted arrest.

When I proceeded to remove his handcuffs, he started screaming, begging me not to take the cuffs off. "Please, please don't do that. Take me to jail. Take me to jail!"

"Then tell me who the f**king punk is now?" I shouted!

"I am! I am!" he replied.

"Are you sure?"

"Yes! Yes! I'm the punk! I'm the punk!"

All the times that I went behind this warehouse, not one time did I ever have to remove the handcuffs.

There was this other time I went into the jail cell area to check on a prisoner who was screaming while hanging on the bars and spitting on the monitor camera.

"Knock it off! Get off the bars and go lay down and keep quiet!"

"F**k you and your mother!" the prisoner shouted back.

An explosion went off inside of me. In the next three seconds I was inside the jail cell, wailing on this guy, with everything I had, with every intention of hurting him bad.

Then the supervisor on duty rushed in with a couple of officers to drag me off this guy.

There were many times I was written up for going far beyond the reasonable amount of force to subdue or arrest somebody. Needless to say, I had the reputation for having a short fuse, of being a walking time bomb. The officers that I worked with on the evening shift loved working with me, loved knowing that when they were in a tight jam, that I was coming to back them up. They also loved seeing my face getting all red and veins popping out of my head, knowing that any second now I was about to explode.

There were other officers who were afraid to work with me. They felt that if they were with me on a call and things got out of control, my temper would get the best of me and then their career would be in jeopardy, along with mine. There were many times somebody was trying to sue the department and the Town of Windsor on account of me.

Over the first eleven years of my career, there were just too many times that my temper flared up, got out of control, and then I would become physically aggressive and hurt somebody.

The Town of Windsor tried dealing with my anger issues by sending me to anger management seminars. The seminars were good as far as filling me with a lot of head knowledge, but unless there's a heart transformation, going to a seminar is not going to work. In a matter of a couple of weeks after attending these seminars, somebody would get in my face and the fight was on.

It was in August of 1984, that I got called into the Chief's office. Chief Patterson said to me, "Carl, one more incident with you and we will have to terminate you. You're nothing but a liability risk."

After my visit to the Chief's office, I knew I was in trouble. There was just no way that I wasn't going to end up losing my temper and hurting somebody. It was just a matter of time.

I still had fourteen years to go to make it to my twenty-five years. I was scared. Fearful! I was married and I had two very young daughters. What was I going to do?

Impossible! No way was I going to finish my career as a Windsor police officer. My back was up against the wall. There was no way out for me!

BUT GOD

But God! *If not for His grace and His mercy being strong enough, more than sufficient (2 Corinthians 12:9)* to make a way where there seemed to be no way, there is no way that I would be alive today. Or maybe I'd be locked up in some prison somewhere, fighting every day just to stay alive.

The thing is, I didn't even know God at the time, but He knew me! *"Before I formed you in your mother's womb, I knew you." (Jeremiah 1:5)*

It was only two months later that I got invited to a healing service in Worcester, MA. Even though I didn't believe that God healed people, I went anyways. Because of my mom, I had some church upbringing. My dad, however, was a devout non-believer!

I also remembered my brother Bruce had this born-again experience with Jesus in 1980. He was always trying to witness to me and get me saved. Only, his words always fell on deaf ears. Little did I know at the time; my brother was planting the seed of salvation.

I believed in a loving God if you behaved, but not when you misbehaved. I believed that there were consequences if you stepped out of line, or if you crossed God in any way.

Anyways, I went to the healing service with a group of friends. One of my friends was Carol. Carol's eyesight was badly affected by Multiple Sclerosis. Due to this dreadful disease everything was a blur for Carol. Her doctor told that there was no cure, that she would have to live with it.

This healing service was held in a big auditorium. The place was packed with people who had every type of affliction imaginable.

The service was led by a little Italian priest named Father D'orio who was preaching on Jesus like I never heard before. He kept repeating, "Jesus is alive! He is here with us! He wants to heal you!"

After preaching that Jesus is alive, he started praying for people.

The lame were leaping out of their wheelchairs, throwing down their crutches and shouting, "I can walk!"

The deaf cried out, "I can hear!"

But I was not buying it. I thought it was all an act. I guess you could say I was a real "Doubting Thomas."

Then he prayed for the blind. He told everyone who was blind to close their eyes and to cover them. Carol was sitting next to me. She did exactly what he had said. Then he prayed that the blind people would see again, and he then ended his prayer, "In Jesus Name…SEE!

My eyes were on Carol at that very moment. When Carol removed her hands from her eyes and opened them, (I'll never, ever, forget that moment), she screamed out, "I can see!"

OMG! I thought. I quickly asked Carol, "Are you kidding? You can actually see?"

"Yes! Yes! I can see!"

That's when everything around me went silent. It was like I was the only one standing there in that packed auditorium!

As I stood there, I felt a presence I cannot put into words. I just knew in my heart that it was Jesus standing before me, asking to come live in my heart.

When you know that God is speaking to you, you don't say "No," but rather, "Yes Jesus. Come and take over my life!"

It says in the *Book of Revelation (3:20): "Behold, I stand at the door to your heart and knock. If any man hear my voice and open the door, I will come into him."*

That's exactly what was happening to me at that very moment. I felt all this anger, bitterness and rage, leave my being. I felt nothing but peace, a peace I never felt before and love and joy that I never experienced…ever! It all came in like a flood.

When I left Worcester that day, I left as a new man! I didn't know anything about being born again or being saved! All I knew at that point was that I was not the same Carl Thomas who woke up that morning. A radical transformation took place in me that day. I was the blind guy who came to Worcester, spiritually blind that is. But God! When I left Worcester, I could see! I could see!

It says in *2 Corinthians (5:17): "If any man be in Christ, he is a new creature, the old things passed away, behold, new things have come."*

I couldn't wait to get home that day and tell everyone I knew what had happened to me—Jesus had come into my heart and He changed me. The first people I wanted to tell were my wife and my two daughters, Melissa and Stephanie. I thought for sure the news would be well received.

I don't remember ever being verbally or physically abusive with my daughters. However, with my first wife it was a different story. I remember many times I became verbally abusive and yes, sometimes it also got physically intimidating.

After I told them what had happened to me in Worcester, my wife said to Melissa and Stephanie, "It's okay girls, daddy is a little bizarre right now."

DISPATCHED BY GOD

When I got to work the next day, I started telling my buddies on the evening shift that Jesus had come into my life and changed me. That didn't go over very well either. "Oh no! Carl is becoming a Jesus freak! This can't be. It won't last!" How wrong they were.

I wasn't losing my temper, nor was I beating up on people any more. They thought I was becoming soft, becoming weak. They wanted the old Carl Thomas. They didn't want this new guy.

They even complained about me to the higher-ups when I would leave Christian reading material with the prisoners. It was never an issue when prisoners were given Hustler or Playboy magazines to pass the time. Only when I would reach out to them and tell them of God's love and transforming power, did it become an issue or a problem (for them, not for me!)

As long as I was doing it on my time, I was not going to stop.

One guy who was locked up for the weekend, spent most of his time reading the magazines I left him. When I came back Monday morning, he told me that over the weekend he had gotten down on his knees, and he prayed the sinner's prayer. He had found it written on the back of one magazine, and he asked Jesus to come into his heart and take over his life. Man, there was no way I was going to stop doing what I was doing.

***

It was in December of 1989, that I arrested a young man running out of Geissler's Supermarket with several stolen cartons of cigarettes. His name was Bill, and he was stealing whatever he could in order to support his heroin addiction. This man was filthy dirty, smelly, with long matted hair, and he was homeless.

When I got Bill to the police station, I let him know that he needed to get help or his life wasn't going to last much longer. I told him that if he would open his heart to Jesus, Jesus could help him change his life for the better.

He looked at me like I had two heads and pretty much told me to mind my own business. I gave him my business card and told him I would be available if he changed his mind and wanted to talk to me.

A few days later on Christmas Eve, Bill was now locked up at the Hartford Detention Center. Everyone at the detention center had someone to call that night. Not Bill. He had no one even remotely interested in his life at that point.

Bill ended up calling me that night. I remember telling him to go get a Bible and to find *Jeremiah* 29:11. It was hard for him to comprehend that God had plans for him. It was also hard to believe that when we give our lives over to Jesus, that all the angels in Heaven rejoice, even over a smelly junkie like himself.

After showing him the scriptures of God's love and His amazing grace for him, I told him it was time to open his heart to Jesus. He thanked me for my time and hung up. Later that night, Bill told me he rolled out of bed, got down on his knees, and he started crying out to Jesus to take over his heart and his life.

Miraculously instead of getting jail time, Bill got accepted into the Youth Challenge program in Hartford, CT. Youth Challenge is a Christ-centered drug rehabilitation program. It not only delivers drug addicts by the Grace of God; it also brings men and women into a very personal and intimate relationship with Jesus.

After doing eighteen months at Youth Challenge, Bill went on to Bible college and got himself a Bachelor's Degree in Biblical Studies. From Bible college, he served as a teacher and administrator at the Youth Challenge program in Florida, where the need was great.

Today, Bill is currently celebrating his 25th wedding anniversary with his beautiful wife, Carmen, his ten grandchildren, and four great grandchildren. Only God! Only God!

Jesus Breaks In

There were these two guys burglarizing my cousin's home in Windsor. A couple other officers and I, surrounded the house and caught these two men coming out the back door. I was the arresting officer.

Since this was my cousin's house they broke into, my fellow officers thought for sure they were going to see the old Carl back in action again. They were looking forward to me exploding on these guys.

Sorry boys, but that's not going to happen. I remember just before putting these two burglars behind bars, I stood with them in the cell block area. I started telling them how Jesus saved me and changed me.

I said, "If He can change me, He can change you."

I went on to tell them that Jesus loved them and died for them on the cross.

As I was speaking of God's love and amazing grace, I noticed tears welling up in their eyes and streaming down their faces. Since I was a newly born-again Christian, I really didn't understand why they were weeping. I didn't know at the time that when we start witnessing to somebody, God's Holy Spirit starts taking over and moving on that person's heart, revealing Himself in a very personal way.

Before I left that night, I left my Bible with them. I told them that I would be back in the morning to pick it up.

When I returned the next day and walked by the cell block area, like music to my ears, I heard one reading Scripture to his buddy who was locked in the adjoining cell.

God truly broke into their hearts that night. I don't know what has become of these two men or where they might be. I think of them often though, and I pray that on that Day, I will meet them again in Heaven.

***

My fellow officers hated me. They rejected me, insulted me, and they ridiculed me. Yet, I was able to find comfort in God's Word.

- *"If the world hates you, keep in mind that it hated me first. If they persecuted me, they will persecute you too." (John 15:18-25)*

- *"Blessed are you when people insult you and persecute you and say all kinds of evil against you because of me." (Matthew 5:11)*
- *"Happy are you if you are insulted because you are Christ followers." (Galatians 1:24)*

These were not just words that I was reading. In all reality this was God speaking to me, comforting me, and encouraging me to keep doing what I was doing.

***

I also want to mention that when I went home from Worcester that day, I went to the many people that I had offended or hurt in some manner—family members, friends, co-workers—and I asked them for their forgiveness. I also went to the ones that offended me or hurt me as well, and I told them that I forgave them.

As for my dad, I loved him but I resented him for the beatings that I and my brothers suffered from him. Yet by God's grace I was able to forgive him as well.

I was liking the new person that I was becoming, but more than that, I was loving the new person that was now living in my heart: the One that was transforming me from the old Carl, to the new Carl!

I've been a Christian now for over three decades. I have to say that it's been the valleys, the storms, and the battles in my journey, that have caused me to grow in my faith in Jesus Christ, and to grow in my love for Him as well.

It was during these tough times that I came to personally experience how real God is. God is faithful. He is personally involved in my life. He cares about my concerns. He is close to me. He is able to make a way where there seems to be no way. I can trust Him, no matter what situation I find myself in.

THOUGH I WALK THROUGH THE VALLEY

I have come to experience His comfort when I have been abandoned or rejected, like when my first wife several years after my conversion gave me an ultimatum, "Jesus or me! You have two weeks to decide." She told me that she felt like I was having an affair…with Jesus!

I tried explaining that Jesus was only making me a better husband, a better father, a better person. She agreed with all of that, yet "I want the man I married, not this new guy."

"But I like this new guy." I protested, "I can't, and I won't, go back to being who I was. I don't need two weeks to decide. It's Jesus!"

Two weeks later, she served me with papers and shortly after that we were divorced. Her attorney told the judge that I belonged to a cult.

I told the judge that I didn't. I said that I simply had a personal relationship with Jesus Christ. I explained to him that Jesus now lives in my heart. Ever since I asked Him into my heart, I've been this new person, a better husband and a better father.

The judge didn't comment.

The divorce also brought separation between me and my two young daughters, Melissa, who was thirteen, and Stephanie, who was eight. I also lost my home.

I remember when Stephanie and I would have these little tea parties in her bedroom, drinking imaginary tea. I remember Melissa riding her bike alongside me as I was training to compete in the 5th Hawaiian Iron Man Triathlon.

We spent so much time together as a family, traveling to Disney World, going to see the Statue of Liberty, even going to Jamaica, climbing Dunn's River Falls. I remember building a tree fort in the backyard for the girls, taking walks with them in the woods behind our home, and going to the park at the end of our street. I was devastated, heartbroken. The divorce turned my world upside down!

39

Carl's daughters Melissa and Stephanie.

I was stripped of everything that I held dear. Did my faith waiver—YES! I was confused and perplexed. *Why was this happening?* I cried a lot. I felt so alone. *God, where are you?* Needless to say, it was a very dark time for me!

But God remained faithful! ! Even when I was doubting Him, He never turned His back on me. As I walked through the valley of the shadow of death, my God was always with me every step of the way. His strength was always there to pick me up off the ground, always there to carry me when I couldn't go another step. His peace, which surpasses all understanding, was always there to guard my heart and my mind.

In addition to all of that, God put it on my heart to forgive my first wife. If it wasn't for God's all sufficient grace, and Him being by my side, I never would have been strong enough to have made it on my own.

Throughout this raging storm in my life, I learned to remain still and to trust in God, that, *"He was working it all out for good in my life"* *(Romans 8:28).*

I only had His Word to stand on. But His word was all I needed to keep me anchored! I learned there is no valley, no darkness, no sorrow, greater than the grace of Jesus. There is no heartbreak that He can't take you through, just like the lyrics to Jason Crabbe's song: "There is nothing greater than grace."

HE IS FAITHFUL

Sure enough, in 1991, two years after my divorce, God took me out of that pit of despair by bringing a beautiful, Christian lady into my life, one whom I immediately fell in love with.

Vicki and I were married a year later, in August of 1992. Not only did He bring Vicki into my life, but He also brought her two precious children, Missy, who was ten years old at the time, and Mark, who was then seven.

Vicki is very special. She is a beautiful sister in Christ, a witness for Jesus more by her actions, than by her words. She has reached out to so many lost souls, by shining God's light, and also by demonstrating God's unconditional love.

It was in the summer of 1995, when after a church service one Sunday morning, Vicki approached a single mom who was eight months pregnant. Jackie was new in the area. She had recently been abandoned by her husband. Even though Vicki really didn't know Jackie very well, it was apparent that Jackie needed help. She had no husband or other family members to help her.

Vicki told Jackie, "If you need me to help you in any way, I'm available." She left Jackie her phone number.

On September 19th, Vicki received a call from Jackie, asking her "Did you really mean what you said?"

Vicki replied, "Of course I did."

"I'm going into labor. Can you please take me to the hospital?" Not only did Vicki take Jackie to the hospital, but she also went into the delivery room to help bring little Zechariah into the world.

A few months after Zech's birth, Jackie needed to return to work. Since Vicki wasn't working at the time and Jackie didn't have family close by, she called on Vicki once again. "Would you be willing to watch my two boys, Zech and Yannick? I will pay you."

Vicki replied, "Sure I'll watch your boys, but I'm not taking any money for doing it."

For the next two and a half years, Zech and Yannick became like our own children, and Jackie became like a sister. Mia familia, forever!

***

Then there was my dad! He was a stroke victim at the time. The only thing he could move was his left arm and he couldn't speak. But he did have a clear mind. The stroke did not affect his mind. Nobody could talk to my dad about Jesus. Nobody!

One day, while Vicki was at home, she felt God speaking to her to go and see my dad at the hospital. God was telling her that He wanted her to share the Gospel message with him. Vicki couldn't imagine going to see her father-in- law and sharing the Gospel with him. Surely, she was hearing things, and it wasn't God.

That day, she didn't go to visit my dad, she stayed home.

On the next day, Vicki again felt God speaking to her, but this time it was much louder. She knew she wasn't hearing things now. She knew it was God! Vicki obeyed Him that day. She went to see him.

My dad loved Vicki. You couldn't help but love Vicki. When she told him the reason she was there, he shook his head no. He didn't want to know God.

Vicki stood her ground, and she told him anyways. As she was talking, she could see that his countenance was changing. She could tell that the Holy Spirit was taking over.

When she was through with her message, she asked him, "Dad, will you pray with me?"

He nodded yes, and he took her hand.

When Vicki got through praying with him, she asked him, "Dad, I need to know, have you accepted Jesus as your personal Lord and Savior?

He took both of her hands in his one big hand, and he placed them over his heart, and then nodded his head, YES.

My refusal, when given the ultimatum of saving my marriage by denying Christ, became the series of events which paved the way for Christ to work in my family and so many others.

***

It was in 1997, that I got a call from my daughter Melissa. She was now married and living in Thousand Oaks, California. "Hi Dad, I just want you to know that I just got through praying, and I have committed my life to following Jesus. I asked Him to come live in my heart. I am now born again!" PRAISE GOD!

It's so true.

- *"God does work all things out for our good, to those who love him."* Romans 8:28
- *"The devil meant to harm me, but God meant it for my good and for the salvation of many."* Genesis 50:20

His Healing Power

I have come to experience His healing power when I was sick. Many years ago, the doctors couldn't stop the swelling in my face as a result of a spider bite. The doctor told Vicki, "If the swelling continues, it will reach the brain stem and your husband will die. He may not make it through the night."

When Vicki came into my hospital room, the look on her face told me that something was terribly wrong. Not one word was said. All we could do was hold each other.

As we held each other, we both felt a presence in my room, the same presence I felt back in Worcester, MA. With God's presence in my room, all we could do was sing praises unto Jesus. One song after another after another.

When the praises stopped, we just knew it didn't matter what the doctor said. Everything was going to be okay.

Sure enough, when I awoke the next morning, the swelling was gone! I was released from the hospital! When the doctors say impossible...that is when Jesus steps in and says, *"With God all things are possible!"*

***

In the year 2010, I was diagnosed with prostate cancer. Vicki and I freaked out. All we could do was hold each other and cry. Why was this happening?

The first diagnosis showed a little bit of cancer. Doctor recommended aggressive monitoring. Twelve months later they snipped off another twelve pieces of my prostate, which showed cancer, but it was not growing. This time though, the doctor wanted to remove the prostate. They were sure that it was just a matter of time before the cancer would spread.

At around the same time, I received a get-well card from Vicki's nine-year-old nephew, John, who lived in Santa Fe, NM. I opened the card and read: "When you read these words, your cancer will be gone!"

I told the doctor to wait and let's see what the third biopsy says. When I had my third biopsy several months later, they put me to sleep and snipped off thirty-two pieces of my prostate, expecting to find more cancer!

Guess what? Even with thirty-two pieces, they found no cancer whatsoever! Praise God!

It's trials like these, and the victories that follow, that all I wanted to do is keep going out as God's witness to my friends, my family, my neighbors, to strangers, and yes, even to my worst enemy and tell them about my GOD!

OTHERS TOUCHED BY THE HAND OF GOD

Jeff was my worst enemy. He hated me so much he planned to ambush me and take me out with a cross-bow. We were thorns in each other's side. I arrested him more times than anybody else and he never went down easy!

One evening, in the center of town, Jeff clobbered this girl over the head with a metal pipe. I was able to find Jeff hiding out at his parent's home. Upon my arrival to the house, Jeff peered through the door to see who was there. When he saw it was me, he tried slamming the door shut. I was able to kick the door in and chase Jeff down the hallway, which led into the kitchen.

Jeff and I fought for several minutes, breaking up the kitchen table and chairs, and anything else that was breakable. Due to the loud commotion, Jeff's parents came from upstairs. As they walked into the kitchen, I was placing handcuffs on their son.

After God saved me, my feelings toward Jeff changed. One night while patrolling around town I saw Jeff stumbling out of a bar. Not only was he intoxicated, but he was also banged up.

Earlier that night, he was attacked by several youths with sticks and bricks. For the very first time, my heart went out to Jeff. I yelled out to him, "Hey Jeff, come over here. Get in my cruiser."

He was in no condition to fight me, so he came over and started to get into the back seat. I said, "No, get in the front seat!"

That night I reached out to Jeff and told him how God had changed me, and that if He can change me, then He can do the same for him.

From that point on, the Holy Spirit took over.

After I was done, I invited him to go to church with me. When I came to pick Jeff up the following Tuesday night to take him to Glory Chapel, he was ready to go to church.

Every week after that, Jeff and his family ended up going to church. He and his entire household got saved! Just as God did a radical transformation in my life, I saw Him do a radical change in Jeff's life as well. Jeff and I are best of friends today. Brothers in Christ forever! ONLY GOD! ONLY GOD!

***

It was in the summer of 1989, that I worked the midnight shift. One of my most frequent areas of patrol was the American Motor Lodge— a place well known for prostitution, drugs, and stolen cars.

As I was driving around the back side of the motel, I noticed a man standing in the doorway to one of the rooms. It was 2:00 a.m., and it was obvious that he had no good reason for being there.

I stopped my cruiser, got out and asked him for ID. I then checked with the dispatcher to see if there were any outstanding warrants for Carlos. Once I determined there was no immediate threat to me, I asked Carlos to sit in my cruiser.

I usually have people sit in the back seat, but I was starting to sense a divine intervention about to take place. Once he sat down, I felt the presence of God immediately take charge of what was about to happen.

The first words out of my mouth were, "Carlos, this might sound strange coming from a police officer, but…God loves you. If you were the only man on earth, Jesus would have left Heaven to die on a cross for your sins, so that you could spend eternity with Him."

Carlos' response was like he was hearing this for the very first time. "Really? God really loves me?" After about an hour of sharing with Carlos God's love for him, I invited him to go to Glory Chapel with me that following Tuesday.

Not only did he accept my invitation, but he went home and invited his girlfriend, Anna, to go as well. Anna didn't believe his story about a cop inviting him to church. But come Tuesday, both Anna and Carlos were ready when I came to pick them up.

The message being preached that night couldn't have been timelier. When Carlos and Anna heard how Jesus left the ninety-nine behind to go out and get the lost sheep, they knew that they were the lost sheep God was coming out to get that night. They both responded to the altar call and committed their lives to the King of kings and the Lord of lords.

Ever since that day, Anna has been very instrumental in the saving of many lives. She is a beautiful witness of God's amazing grace.

Today you will find her singing in the choir at Crossroads Community Cathedral. You will also find her son, Rey, being instrumental in the saving of many broken homes and marriages through his dance ministry.

Rey has told me recently that he and his wife Glendaly are being considered to have their ministry go international aboard the Royal Caribbean Cruise Lines in February 2020. They will be leading the dance and marriage classes for Christian couples sailing with them. He's also an integral core leader in the Strong Enough Men's Retreat. As for Carlos, he has a wheelchair ministry in Santo Domingo, bringing the disabled to our Lord Jesus Christ.

Only God! Only God can take a person out of the muck and mire of life, bring them into His glorious light, and transform them into a mighty witness of God's amazing grace and unconditional love!

The American Motor Lodge

Like I said earlier, the American Motor Lodge was known for its prostitution, drugs, and stolen cars. It also housed many families on State Aid. During the day and into the early evening hours, there were always a bunch of little kids playing and running around in the parking lot. The parking lot became their playground. They had nowhere else to go.

Before Jesus came into my life, I felt nothing toward these kids. When I would patrol through the area, I would sometimes yell at them to go play somewhere else. I also became very angry and judgmental toward the single moms that were doing whatever they could to raise them.

"Why can't they go out and get a job like everybody else? Why does my tax dollar have to go to support them?" Let's just say I copped a real bad attitude every time I drove through there.

BUT GOD! AND ONLY GOD! When Jesus came into my heart with all of His love and compassion, I started seeing others through God's eyes, not through my own eyes anymore. His unconditional love became a natural out-flow into the lives of others, no matter who they were, or what they'd done. As a result of His radical transformation in my life, my heart was moved with compassion toward these families.

What can I do to help them? Whenever I patrolled through the area, I would stop and talk to the kids, befriending them. I would let them sit in my cruiser and turn on the siren. Sometimes I would get out for a few minutes and play hopscotch, or jump rope, or pass the football with the boys. Whatever it took to show them the love of Jesus, that's what I did.

Then one day God put it on my heart to take these kids to Glory Chapel along with their moms, and whoever else wanted to go.

I prayed: "That's a great idea, Lord, but how am I going to get them there?"

At a Bible study I was attending every week, I shared with the group what God had spoken to me. The answer to my prayer came immediately! Pam and Nick, a beautiful couple in the Lord, shouted, "You can borrow our van!"

Since one van was not enough, Jeff, the guy that wanted to ambush me with a cross bow, volunteered to help me with transportation. He went out and bought a used mini-van.

Every Tuesday evening, we would pick up as many kids as we could, and we would bring them to Glory Chapel. There was one-time when Glory Chapel brought church to the American Motor Lodge. Pastor Paul Ecktenkamp brought with him several men and women that were going through the Youth Challenge Program. Outside, in the back-parking lot, we had church! Everybody who was residing at the motel came out of their rooms when they heard the people from Glory Chapel singing and praising God.

What a beautiful sight it was. What a glorious sound it was when everybody came together and started singing and praising God. After the singing and praising, the men and women from the program started sharing their testimonies of how God was delivering them from their drug addictions, and whatever other addictions they were having.

- *"By the blood of the Lamb and the words of their testimony I will draw all man unto Me." (Rev.12:10-11)*

That's exactly what happened that night. I saw prostitutes, drug addicts, people whose lives were shattered for one reason or another, all being drawn to the Lord, calling on Jesus to save them.

- *"God has chosen the foolish things, the despised things, the weak things of the world, and the debased things of the world." (1 Cor.1:27-28)*

With God it just doesn't matter!

Robert

Robert was a beautiful example of God's amazing grace. Robert was a young and very handsome teenage boy, strung out on drugs, wild parties, friends galore, and always getting himself arrested on various misdemeanor charges. The times that I was Robert's arresting officer, my heart always went out to him.

When looking at Robert, I was able to see him through God's eyes. I saw him as a lost soul, with a great need to be loved. I took Robert under my wing with every intention of steering him in the right direction. After work I would bring him to my home, where he was more than welcomed by Vicki and her two children, especially Missy.

On Sundays, he would go to church with us. One Sunday morning, God got a hold of his heart and saved him at the altar. Robert had a genuine born-again experience. For the next several weeks, Robert had no desire for drugs, or alcohol, or wild parties. His desire was to walk the straight and narrow path and serve God every chance he had.

After several weeks passed, we weren't seeing or hearing from Robert. Vicki and I started to worry about where he could be. It was soon after that a Bloomfield police officer found Robert in a field sitting in his truck, dead from a drug overdose. Robert had become like family to us. We were devastated!

I was asked to give the eulogy at Robert's funeral by his family members. God had a slightly different plan. He was sending me there to preach the Gospel. I was a bit nervous about preaching the Gospel. Most of these people were non-Christians, certainly not there to hear me preach. Some were probably getting high right there at the funeral home.

Vicki went with me, of course, along with our pastor, Pastor Gary. When we got there, the room was filled to capacity. When I got up to preach, miraculously, all the nervousness went away.

"Robert came into a personal relationship with Jesus Christ when he asked Jesus into his heart and life. Because of his faith in God, you can be sure he is in Heaven right now. Just because he messed up in those final hours of his life doesn't mean that he didn't make it!"

"In Heaven there's a banquet table, where in the last days a great feast will be served. All those who have put their faith in Jesus will be sitting at this table. You can be sure that Robert will be one of them, with Jesus sitting at the head."

"If you want to be there as well, if you want to see Robert again, then I invite you to come to the front of the room. Pastor Gary and I will pray with you. Come! Ask Jesus to forgive you for your sins. Put your faith in Him by asking Him to come into your heart, to be the Lord of your life. Confess Him as your Lord, believe with all your heart that He has risen from the dead and that He lives."

For the next few moments nobody moved.

Total silence.

Then, Robert's grandfather got up out of his seat, and with his cane limped down toward me. Then I saw Robert's dad get up and do the same. Then another, and another, and another!

Everybody, I mean everybody, made their way to the front of the room! GOD, ONLY GOD, saved everybody that was there that day to say their last goodbyes to Robert, knowing that one day they will see their friend again sitting at the banquet table with Jesus sitting at the head.

Billy

Then there was Billy. It was February 7, 1985, when I met Billy Walters at the other end of my shotgun. "Freeze, or I will shoot!" I meant it! You see, only a few hours earlier, Billy had broken into a house in Southwick, MA.

While he and his girlfriend were still in the house, the homeowner came home. When the homeowner entered the house, Billy took him by surprise and drove a twelve-inch knife into the man's stomach! After stabbing the owner, Billy and his girlfriend fled the scene in the homeowner's car. Billy drove to Windsor, where he and his girl hid out in the girlfriend's home. Her dad, a retired police officer, and her mom, weren't home at the time.

I was on patrol that night. When I got the call, the dispatcher advised that two burglary suspects with a knife, and a possible gun, were hiding out at this residence.

Upon my arrival, the house was already surrounded with Windsor, Hartford, and Connecticut State Police, along with police canine and helicopters hovering overhead. I took up my position behind the house, covering the back door with my shotgun loaded, and with one round chambered.

State Police, who had taken charge over the scene used a bullhorn to convince Billy and his girlfriend to come out with their hands up. In what seemed to be a long time, the girl came out the back door with her hands held high, screaming, "I surrender! I surrender!" She was immediately apprehended and removed from the scene.

About an hour later, I saw Billy sneaking out the back door. It appeared to me that he didn't intend to surrender, but rather to escape somehow. I yelled to him to freeze or I would shoot! Billy froze for a moment, but in the blink of an eye, he turned and ran back into the house.

At this time the decision was made to go into the house with police canine. Once we entered the house, it was only moments later that Billy came out from hiding with his hands high in the air. He was immediately apprehended and taken to Hartford, where he was locked up for the rest of the weekend.

The following Monday morning, Billy was transported to the Windsor Courthouse to be arraigned. While in route to the courthouse, Billy was able to uncuff himself with a handcuff key he had hidden under his tongue. When Billy had been hiding out at the house, his girlfriend gave him a handcuff key that belonged to her father.

When the van pulled up in front of the courthouse, the driver, who weighed over 300 pounds, went to the rear of the van to open the door. Upon opening it, Billy, who weighed maybe 145 pounds, jumped out of the van and fled the scene on foot.

I was immediately dispatched to the scene, along with our police canine unit. Canine Officer Banasiak led the way to a wooded area overlooking the Farmington River.

Our dog found Billy hiding under a log. I was the arresting officer.

When it was just me and Billy at the station house, I heard God's still small voice in my heart saying, "Tell him. Tell him."

Tell him what Lord?

"Tell him that I love him and that I died for him."

But Lord, this guy just stabbed somebody. He's a real bad dude. He isn't going to listen to me. He'll laugh in my face.

That still small voice became a little louder, "TELL HIM!"

Yes, Lord!

"Billy, I have something to tell you. God loves you! And he died for you on an old rugged cross."

No sooner did the words leave my mouth, his eyes welled up with tears streaming down his face.

"What's the matter Billy? Why are you crying?"

"Nobody ever told me that they love me, not even my father, nor my mother. Now a Windsor cop is telling me that God loves me?"

"Yes, Billy and I love you too."

ONLY GOD!

It was a short time later while visiting Billy at Somers State Prison, that I lead Billy to the Lord. Right before my very eyes, I saw the old Billy die and a new Billy come alive!

Billy was a stellar inmate, but more so a stellar witness for the Lord.

- *"God demonstrates His own love for us, in that while we were yet sinners, while we were his enemies, Christ died for us." (Romans 5:8)*

Two years later, it was time for Billy to do his time in Massachusetts for the stabbing in Southwick. I went to court with Billy to be a character witness. Every newspaper, every radio, and TV news station was there to cover Billy's story.

I didn't know what I was going to say, but when I stood up the words came flowing out.

"Your Honor, I'm not here to get you to reduce Billy's sentence, nor am I here to be a character witness for Billy Walters. I'm here to be a witness for Jesus Christ. Because of Jesus, Billy is not the same man today that he was two years ago. When Billy prayed and asked Jesus into his heart, Jesus came in and did a radical change in this man's life. He's a new man today, a beautiful man, and if God can change Billy, He can change anyone here! Thank you, your Honor."

- *"When it's time for you to speak, God will fill your mouth with the words that you are to speak." (Luke 12:12)*

I just want to add that when I went to court that day, I went dressed in my police uniform. By the time I got back to Windsor, the prosecutor had already called my captain.

She screamed at him, "Why is one of your police officers coming up here and turning my courthouse into an evangelistic meeting?"

I received a verbal reprimand for wearing my uniform.

Billy got a 15-year sentence at Gardner, Massachusetts. While attending chapel services at the prison, he went up to the volunteer, Wayne, and told him about this police officer down in Connecticut. He told him how this officer had a big impact on his life.

Wayne called me and asked me if I would be willing to come to Gardner and share my testimony with the inmates.

The drive to North Central Correctional Institute is approximately eighty miles long. After driving about an hour and a half, I turned down this long, dark, and winding driveway leading to the prison.

It was a wintery evening, so it was hard to see where I was going. Finally, I could see the prison in the distance. It was like a scene from a horror film. This prison was once a mental institution. Now, with high fences wrapped in razor wire and several old brick buildings, this place was downright eerie and frankly made me feel very uncomfortable.

Immediately, I started praying. "Lord, you better be real, because if you're not, I really don't want to be here."

Saturday, October 11, 1986   Journal Inquirer   Page 2

Living

The prisoner:
'I didn't feel afraid when I was walking back to the block'

EDITOR'S NOTE: These two stories constitute the third and final report on the conversion experiences of born-again Christians.

By GUTHRIE SAYEN
Journal Inquirer Staff Writer

Bill Walters was terrified of being raped by a much bigger inmate at Somers State Prison. So he got a knife.

That same day, Carl Thomas, a Windsor policeman, came to visit Thomas, and Walters had begun to look to Jesus for understanding.

The prisoner told the cop about the big man and the precaution taken. The cop said it was time to accept Christ.

Walters confessed his sins aloud. It took a good hour. Though only 24, Walters had been in jail at least a half-dozen times before, and this time he probably won't be released till he's in his mid-30s.

"I asked Jesus. Please come into my heart because I am weak and I need you now," Walters says.

"Afterward I felt like a big weight had just been lifted from me. When I left the visiting room, I had a bounce to my walk and a big smile on my face, and I didn't feel afraid when I was walking back to the block."

In his cell, Walters dumped the knife in the toilet and flushed. Then he prayed to Jesus that he be transferred to another block.

A half-hour later, he was, "They just told me to pack my stuff."

Walters, formerly of Windsor Locks, claims his commitment to Jesus has turned his life around. Dianne Dillon doubts it.

"A lot of people find Jesus in jail. Unfortunately, they leave him there at their release date," says the assistant district attorney from Massachusetts. She cites the case she recently prosecuted against Walters.

On Feb. 27, 1986, Walters broke into a house in Southwick, Mass., and drove a 12-inch knife into the

Born-again Christians

owner's stomach, nearly killing him.

Dillon says Walters, who admits the crime, did not change his plea from innocent to guilty until after she had presented the state's case in court. She also says that Walters, who was already talking about Jesus, threatened witnesses and President Reagan.

"I find it somewhat inconsistent to say you're born again while you're threatening people at the same time," Dillon says.

Walters admits to backsliding. "Things were going all right until I realized I was going to get some serious time. I felt like I was losing everything. I think what I was going through at that time was growing pains. At some point the Lord is going to test us."

He says he confessed his sins and feels he is forgiven. As for Dillon, he says, "I pray that she finds that light that I have found."

Whatever he has found, it has cost him a lot of trouble finding it.

Walters says he was forced to leave Windsor Locks High School in the middle of the ninth grade after being falsely accused of stealing drugs. From then on he was continually in trouble.

He admits a succession of burglaries and thefts committed to pay for his addiction to marijuana and alcohol. In the early '80s, he served nearly four years in

prison. "When I got out in '84, I knew I'd be coming back."

Last year, more burglaries and escapes landed him at Somers, the state's maximum security prison. When he finishes his bid there, it's on to Walpole State Prison in Massachusetts for the bungled job in Southwick.

After his arrest following the stabbing, he attempted to escape. It was Thomas who captured him. While being held at the Windsor lockup, the cop lent the criminal a book on Christianity.

"When I was reading the book, it was like seeing aspects of my life. I started crying. Everything was coming out of me like I had nothing left. It felt good in a way. I didn't feel I had any pressure or all the built-up hostility inside me."

But in prison the pressure built up again. "It was like everything that I said to Jesus and everything I had read just went away. I started sinking into another depression.

"So I wrote Carl Thomas a letter saying I was going to escape, and I asked him to blow me away if he saw me running because he was the only friend I had, the only person I could call a friend."

Thomas came to the rescue, calming him down, visiting him weekly if he could and sending a letter if he couldn't. Though he admits to setbacks, Walters says

Bill Walters

his faith is so strong that he plans to be a minister when he gets out of prison.

"Not only would I give my life for God. I would give my life for Carl Thomas — just as I know he would give his life for mine."

JI PHOTO BY ADRIAN KEATING

The cop:
'That compassion in me — God — told me to reach out'

By DOREEN HOOD
Journal Inquirer Staff Writer

After Officer Carl Thomas joined the Windsor Police Department 14 years ago, he turned into a tough, cynical cop.

"I tried very hard to present a macho image to everybody," says Thomas, 35. "I had a bad temper, a short fuse. I was very prideful. It got the job a lot of 'trouble.' The louder his police work, and colleagues avoided him because of his temper.

But two years ago, after joining a fellow officer at a healing service in Worcester, Mass., Thomas found God. He had a born-again experience that he says changed his life and brought him a new perspective to his work.

Because he is a cop, Thomas's spiritual life and professional life sometimes conflict. The drastic change in his personality has got him raised reviews from his colleagues.

Carl Thomas

Thomas, who was raised a Roman Catholic, went to church every Sunday and said his prayers regularly. "But it was all up here," he says, pointing to his head. "It wasn't in my heart."

He calls his born-again experience a personal commitment to Jesus Christ. "It's like the old you dies. You re-live a little baby."

As a police officer, Thomas says he is to show compassion to contact those who may need faith the most — prisoners.

One of those is Bill Walters. Walters had a companion had stolen a car to Windsor, driven to Southwick, Mass., and gone on a burglary spree that included the near-fatal stabbing of one man. Walters was eventually picked up in Windsor.

Thomas was the arresting officer. While processing Walters, Thomas says: "That compassion in me — God — told me to reach out to Bill Walters.

While Walters was held in the Windsor lockup, Thomas chatted with him about Christianity and

gave him a book. That was the beginning of a friendship that led to Walters' conversion, which Thomas says has reformed Walters.

Walters, who is serving time in Somers State Prison on another burglary charge, was recently sentenced to 12 to 15 years for the Southwick stabbing. Thomas testified in uniform on Walters' behalf.

"I want to stress that I did not go to court to ask that Bill Walters' sentence be reduced," Thomas says. "What he did was a terrible act of violence and destruction, and he should have to pay for what he has done." Thomas wanted to explain that finding Jesus Christ has helped Walters start a new life.

But Thomas' new faith and actions have not been well received by everyone on the job, and he acknowledges he has made some mistakes. In his zeal to tell fellow officers about Jesus, he alienated some people. "Right afterwards I became real hyper, real gung-ho

about it."

Some of Thomas' fellow officers fear his new outlook has softened him and lessened his effectiveness. Others fear his testimony for Walters might make it seem that police and prosecutors are in opposing camps.

Chief Marie Patterson reprimanded Thomas for appearing in uniform while off duty and told him to refrain from talking to anyone about religion while he is on duty.

While that request is difficult for him, Thomas says "I'll do whatever my employer asks of me." And he agrees that testifying in uniform was a mistake.

But Thomas maintains he is a better cop since being born again. He says he has learned compassion for everyone, including prisoners. But he adds, he would not hesitate to fire his gun if his or a fellow officer's life were in danger.

"Some of them say they want the old 'Carl Thomas back," he says of colleagues. "But I really enjoy my life now."

JI PHOTO BY MIKE KOKOSKA(?)
Carl Thomas

Before being born again,

North Central Correctional Institute, Gardner, Massachusetts.

NORTH CENTRAL CORRECTIONAL INSTITUTE

When I finally got there, the room was filled with over a hundred prisoners waiting to hear my testimony. BUT GOD! When I got up to speak, a calm came over me.

When I opened my mouth, the words came flowing out speaking of God's love and His amazing grace in my life.

I told them, "If He can change me, He can change you!"

Thirty years, and I am still going to Gardner every 2nd Sunday, and 4th Tuesday of each month, still preaching God's love and amazing grace.

- *"You just never know what God is going to do next. Eye has not seen, nor ear heard, nor has entered the heart of man, what God has in store for those who love Him." (1 Cor 2:9)*

- *"God is able to do exceedingly abundantly more than we could ever ask or think." (Eph 3:20)*

Never did I think, as a police officer, that I would be doing prison ministry. Wayne was a total stranger to me. Now he is one of my dearest brothers in the Lord. We've been serving God together for three decades, and we're still going strong.

Over the years, God has blessed us with four more brothers—Tom, Mark, Gene and Dale. Whenever one of us gets up to preach, it's always about Christ and him crucified.

***

Retirement

It really doesn't matter how long I've been a follower of Jesus, or how many times I've been doing prison ministry, or how many people I've witnessed to. The storms and the battles keep coming.

It's really no different for the believer than it is for the non-believer. The only difference is as a believer in Christ, I never had to go it alone. Jesus was always, and will always, be by my side to take me through.

It was 1995, twenty-two years into my police career, that I was forced to retire from the police department. I remember working undercover at the time, involved in a drug bust. After completing the operation, and all the suspects were in custody, my heart started beating really fast. I was feeling very weak, and finding it very hard to breathe. Since everything was under control, I left the scene and drove myself to the hospital. This was a foolish move on my part, BUT GOD got me there safe and sound.

When I arrived, my heart was still beating very fast. The heart monitor showed 200 beats per minute. The doctors were amazed that I didn't have a stroke or a heart attack. An arrhythmia specialist advised me that I had a tachycardia, an electrical malfunction in the heart's ventricles. They did a procedure called an oblation, where they go into the heart and burn out the area that caused the problem.

Since this problem is caused by too much stress, and the adrenaline rush which is very common in police work, I was told by my doctor that I would have to retire. There was no guarantee that it was not going to happen again. "Maybe next time, you won't make it to the hospital where we could save you."

I wasn't ready to retire! BUT GOD obviously had other plans for me, and He wasn't going to let a heart attack, or a stroke, get in the way of His plan for my life.

I was about seven years into my prison ministry, and still going strong. Every time I went up there, I still felt the presence of God. Each time I'd go to bring a word of encouragement to the inmates, I too, ended up being encouraged by them.

I remember one Sunday afternoon; I was asked to minister to an inmate who was locked up in a padded cell. When I first got there, the only way I could talk to him was through a small opening in the bottom of the door. I couldn't even see the man's face. The guards told me it was for my own safety.

"There's no way I can speak to this man this way. You're going to have to unlock the door and let me inside with him."

To my surprise, they unlocked the door and let me inside, and then they shut the door behind me. At no time while I was inside with this young man, did I feel that my life was in danger, nor did I feel threatened in any way. I knew God was with me for sure!

The inmate looked at me as though I was the crazy one. He appeared to be somewhat jumpy, uneasy, and suspicious of my being there. I told him who I was and why I was there. I let him know that he can have a peace and a calm in his life and know that somebody loves him and forgives him. That someone is able to set him free from the prison that is within him.

"Who is this someone?" he asked.

"This Someone is Jesus," I replied. "He is here right now, knocking on the door of your heart. If you ask Him to come in, He will, and he will be with you forever. You'll never have to fear, or be afraid of anything, ever again. He promises that He will never leave you nor forsake you, that He will always be there to help you. You will always be able to go forth with confidence, knowing that there's nothing man can do to you."

As I continued to minister with God's anointing, I saw this man's countenance change from someone very disturbed, to a man of peace, with a calmness coming over him.

It was like Jesus, standing there speaking to the stormy seas, "*Peace be still!*," and a calmness came over the waters.

I asked him, "Would you like to pray with me? Open the door to your heart and ask Jesus to come in?"

"Yes," he said. We held hands and prayed.

RETURN TO VIETNAM

The year was 2005. I went to a Promise Keepers' convention to listen to Dave Roever preach the Word of God in upper state New York. Roever was with the U.S. Navy in Vietnam. He was severely burned when a white phosphorous grenade exploded in his hand. He was thought to be dead.

Dave shares his inspiring story of triumph over tragedy through Jesus Christ all over the world. When Dave was done speaking, he asked if there were any Vietnam Vets in the audience who were willing to return to Vietnam to share God's love, to preach Christ and Him crucified.

He was looking for a team of vets to return to a nation, not with a M-16, but with John 3:16:

- *"For God so loved the world that He sent His only begotten Son that whosoever believes in him shall not perish but have everlasting life."*

That included the Nation of Vietnam.

I knew of Dave Roever and his amazing story. He had my utmost respect and admiration. His messages have always inspired me, especially when going through my own trials and tragic situations. Going with Dave Roever into battle in the spiritual realm, was like going into battle with another Green Beret in the physical realm. After the service was over, I went over to Roever's table and signed up for the mission.

Shortly thereafter, I went back to Vietnam with a team of Vietnam vets, with Dave Roever leading the way. We covered a lot of territory, from Saigon, to the Central Highlands, to the northern parts of the country.

We traveled mostly by bus into the villages and mainly to the orphanages. A lot of the children in Vietnam are homeless, and without families to love them.

We went to pour out God's love for them, and gift them with things like bicycles and tricycles.

I remember on the last day of our journey, we were inside this large compound that housed many children.

I remember being in a big circle, holding hands, singing and praising God, when I saw a large bus driving through the gate and coming to a stop just inside the compound. Dave Roever instructed the team to walk over to the bus.

When the bus unloaded the passengers, it became very apparent to me that the men standing in front of us were our very worst enemy, the North Vietnamese, the Viet Cong, "Charlie!"

My initial reaction to these men standing in front of me was utter contempt. All I wanted to do was turn around and walk away.

God's word says that: *"We are to love our enemy."* (Matthew 5:44)

I've come to realize over the years that with God's Word, there are no exceptions. As for me, at that very moment, the men I was standing face to face with, were an exception to God's Word! I hated these people!

I prayed: "Jesus, if You want me to love them, then You're going to have to love them through me."

As soon as I prayed that prayer, I felt God's Holy Spirit rising up inside of me, washing away the hate, and replacing it with His love. In a moment's time, I was walking towards these men.

With all of God's love and amazing grace I was embracing them, forgiving them, and being embraced and forgiven as well. God did a divine intervention in my heart that day. ONLY GOD! ONLY GOD!

From the very first day God saved me in that big auditorium in Worcester, MA, He has been working on me ever since, and will continue to work on me, *"until the Day of Christ Jesus."* (Philippians 1:6)

God wasn't only sending me back to Vietnam to touch hearts for Him. He was sending me back to touch my heart as well. He wanted to purge it of the bitterness and unforgiveness that still lingered very deep inside.

KEEPING ON

After fifteen years of security work post retirement, I was able to stop working and devote more time to helping my siblings take care of our mom and dad. Mom was suffering from a few medical issues, along with vascular dementia. Dad was only seventy-five years old when he had his stroke in 1996. He passed away in May of 2010. Mom passed away in January 2012. God made it clear that caring for my mom and dad was exactly what He wanted me to be doing.

In September 2015, I went back to work for the Town of Windsor. For the last three and a half years, I've been driving a mini-bus, transporting senior citizens to their diverse appointments. I love my job! God gives me opportunities every day to witness, to fellowship, and to praise Him and worship Him with others. Many of my passengers call my bus, the Holy Bus!

Though I have failed so many times, I've always tried to walk the talk before all of my children, and Vicki as well.

- *"If we do not provide for our own, especially for those of our own household, then we have denied the faith, and are worse than an unbeliever." (1 Timothy 5:8)*

In addition to my immediate family, God has used me with extended family members as well. My cousin Robbie was seven years older than me. I always looked up to him as though he was my big brother.

In later years, this big tough "brother" of mine developed some kind of kidney disease. This required dialysis twice a week for the rest of his life, if he didn't receive a new kidney. Before Christ, as much as I loved my cousin, giving him one of my kidneys wouldn't even have been a thought.

Living for myself had been a big priority in my life. However, with Jesus, living for others becomes the big priority in our lives. The only way Jesus is manifested through us is when we are willing to deny self, willing to lay down our lives, so that others may live. The only way this is accomplished is by the grace of God.

I say this, because I don't want this story to be about me and what I did. This story is to be about Jesus, and His amazing grace, working in us and through us.

As I watched Robbie with this disease, struggling each week to stay alive and live a somewhat normal life, I was moved with compassion. It became very clear what God was calling me to do.

In November 2004, Robbie and I went to Hartford Hospital. By the grace of God, Robbie was given one of my kidneys, and lived out a quality of life until his passing in 2013.

***

There have been many times since I retired from the police department that I've thought there might be more that God wanted me to do, in addition to my prison ministry and family. I thought there might be more lives to touch, more places to go where He could use me to minister His love, preach the Good News, share my testimony, and lead others to Christ.

I remember when Crossroads Community Cathedral was asking for volunteers to go to Guatemala. *Yes, Lord, send me!* I thought for sure He was answering my prayer and sending me to Guatemala.

About a month before leaving on this great missionary trip, I ended up in the hospital due to a fast and irregular heartbeat. The same heart rate that forced me to retire from the police department. The chances of this happening in the jungles of Guatemala was just too risky. The Lord made it very clear that He was not sending me!

"Ok Lord, if going to Gardner twice a month and ministering to my family and other people in my own backyard is all that you have for me, then that's fine. Your Word says to be content in all things. So,

I shall be content and thankful for all that you are doing in me, and for all that you are doing through me."

The Lord knows my heart's desire is to touch as many lives as I can for His namesake and for His glory. If He has more for me to do, that would be great. If not, that's okay too. He calls the shots, not me.

I've come to realize as a follower of Christ, our story keeps on keeping on. God, and only God, will bring it to completion on that Day He decides to call us home.

**

One Sunday morning in March 2018, I responded to an altar call. Even though I've been a Christian, following Jesus for more than three decades, I was struggling.

Like the Apostle Paul:

- *"The good that I wish, I do not do, but I practice the very evil that I do not wish." (Romans 7:19)*

I don't normally go to the altar for prayer. However, that one Sunday, I went to the altar, got down on my knees, and silently cried out to Jesus for help.

As I knelt there for several minutes, weeping before the Lord, I felt this hand placed on my shoulder. When I finally got up and turned around, I saw that it was a brother that I met two years ago at a Strong Enough Men's Retreat. Bob made a very positive impression on me at that retreat. Like King David, he was truly a man after God's own heart.

Without even giving it a second thought, I blurted out, "Bob, I need an accountability partner. Will you be that partner?"

Without any hesitation, he replied, "Sure I will. Not a problem."

For the next several weeks, Bob and I met once a week for breakfast. It was always a joy to sit down with Bob. He is a very down to earth kind of guy, one who has stuff in his life that he struggles with as well.

Sometimes I think I'm the only follower of Christ struggling. There must be something wrong with me. Then you start to isolate yourself from the Body of Christ. That's exactly where the enemy wants you to be, and it's what he wants you to think. The enemy is nothing but a liar, and a false accuser of the brethren.

I opened up to Bob about the things I was struggling with. As I did, I felt a cleansing, a purging going on inside me.

Like David in Psalm 40:

- *"I cried onto the Lord, He heard my cry at the altar that one Sunday morning, and lifted me out of the horrible pit, out of the miry clay and set my feet back on solid ground and put a new song in my heart."*

This is what was happening to me. Praise God! My time with Bob was not just a time of cleansing and purging, it was also a time of great fellowship. We shared so many stories and testimonies of what God has done, and what He is now doing, in our lives.

I shared with Him about my blind friend and what happened at Worcester. I shared about the cop I was before Jesus came into my heart, and the cop I became after Jesus took over my life. We talked about my prison ministry. I told him about what God is doing in my life now.

After sharing story after story, Bob invited me to go to a Strong Enough Men's Retreat that was coming up in November.

My initial reply to Bob's invitation was, "No thanks, Bob. I don't think that I'm going to have the time."

Bob is also the kind of guy that doesn't like taking "No" for an answer.

"Listen Carl, I would love for you to be one the three speakers giving your story to the retreatants."

Well, that certainly changed things. I'm always willing to make myself available to share my story, giving Jesus all the honor and glory for the great things He has done in my life.

My answer was, "Yes, Bob. I would love to do it!"

Wow! This is so awesome! Thank you, Jesus, for giving me another venue to share with sixty men at one time, of the wondrous things that my God has done in my life!

Little did I know, God had much more in store for me. After giving a very condensed version of my story to the retreatants that one Saturday morning in November, I was approached by another core leader of Strong Enough Ministries. Actually, Bob Wilson is the person who had a vision and started Strong Enough Ministries several years ago.

He said to me, "Carl, you have a great story, especially in the way it relates to the police. Your story is definitely a book and maybe even a movie."

Bob went on to tell me that he knows this book publisher who has a personal connection with a movie producer who specializes in Christian-based movies. With my story, these books and films would minister to churches, police, military, and prisoners all over the country.

The publisher and producer have read my story and they agreed. They are very excited that my story has the potential of reaching many thousands of people for the Lord Jesus Christ and for the salvation of so many more!

Never could I have ever imagined that God would use my story in a book, or on a movie screen, to minister to so many thousands across the land. ONLY GOD! ONLY GOD!

I don't know exactly what tomorrow holds for me as I type out the words to my story, but I know Who is holding my tomorrow, and the whole rest of my future. Will my witness for Jesus end with a book, and a movie, I don't know? What I do know is that I serve an amazing God, and with God, I've learned not to put any limitations or restrictions on Him.

- *"I serve a God Who is able to do exceedingly abundantly more than I could ever ask or think." (Ephesians.3:20)*

As I look back on all that He has accomplished through me to others, I can proclaim that my story with Christ Jesus has been an amazing journey. Without Jesus leading the way, there would not be any journey. Without His grace, and His love, and His Holy Spirit living inside me, there's no way I could have done all the things that I have mentioned since that very first day I gave my life to Christ in Worcester until now.

- *"It was all God working in me to will and to work for His good pleasure." (Philippians 2:13)*

- *"From that very first day it was no longer I who lived, but Jesus who lived inside me." (Gal. 2:20)*

- *"He came to seek and to save the lost" (Luke 19:10)*

Since Jesus lives inside me, it was all Jesus seeking and saving all those lost souls that I encountered along the way. I was just the vessel, the instrument in His hands. My story is not about me, it's all about my Savior, my Lord, my Jesus! To Him be all the Praise and Honor, and Glory!

Amen!

EPILOGUE

Today, Vicki continues to be that light God sent my way almost 28 years ago. She has truly been an example of God's steadfast love, grace, and mercy in my life.

The work of Christ is being worked out in us, and through us. mostly to our children and their wonderful spouses, as well as our amazing grandchildren! We are so blessed that all our kids, spouses included, are living very successful lives. My Melissa is a retired cop, Stephanie a production manager. Vicki's Melissa is a high school Vice Principal, and Mark a history teacher.

Carl and his family.
From left to right: Melissa, Missy on the bottom, then Stephanie and Mark.

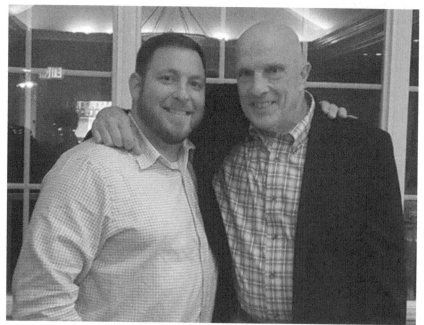

Carl and his nephew Joshua.

Joshua knocked on deaths door a couple of times. You see, he was an heroin addict. Everybody said impossible! Vicki and I would not give up on him because we knew that with God all things are possible! Praise God Joshua has been clean for the last three and a half years and is now a very successful Landscape Architect.

I still have personal contact with Carlos, Jeff, and Bill. These men and their families, are still serving God today, with their own story of Gods amazing grace and transforming power through our Lord and Savior Jesus Christ. As for Billy, he has gone to be with Lord. He was a man mightily used by God for the salvation of many lost souls. The last time I saw, or heard from Kenny, was the day we prayed in that small room in Enfield, CT.

Prison ministry is stronger than ever. I'm still driving up that long, winding driveway, that leads to those old brick buildings. However, I am no longer questioning how real God is. He is very real! There's been a couple occasions that Vicki and the other wives have gone into the prison to minister as well. However, for the most part Vicki, stays behind the scenes and prays for me. I sometimes wonder where I would be today without my praying wife. Vicki and I are both praying that my story will touch the lives of many with God's amazing grace.

Today we sit in awe of what God is able to do in all of our lives, if we would just surrender our lives into His hands. Actually, He is able to do exceedingly, abundantly, more than we could ever ask or think.

If you have just read this book or have just seen this movie I believe that Jesus is reaching out to you right now. He wants you to know personally of His Amazing Grace and Awesome Love; and His power to transform your life. If He is knocking on to the door of your heart, now is the time to open the door and invite Him in. He has been with me ever since that day I invited Him into my heart in that big auditorium back in Worcester, Mass. He has never left me, nor has He ever forsaken me.

Today is the day to take a step of Faith: Confess with your mouth Jesus as your Lord; and believe with your heart that God raised Him from the dead...and you will be saved. John 3:16 says that God so loved the world (that means you) that He gave His only begotten Son (Jesus); that whoever believes in Him shall not perish but have eternal life.

On that day when you take your last breath here on earth, you can know that in a twinkling of an eye you will be standing face to face with God, and that is for all eternity

If you are at a loss for words, then with all your heart pray these words:

> *Lord Jesus I am a sinner.*
> *You died on the cross, shedding Your precious*
> *blood to wash away my sin.*
> *I receive You this day and what You did for me*
> *so that I could spend eternity with You!*
> *Come into my heart now Lord Jesus.*
> *Lead me and guide me for the whole rest of my life.*
> *In Your name I pray.*

IMAGES FROM THE MOVIE

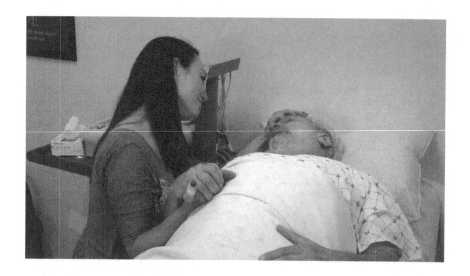

You've read the book, now see the movie!

www.PoliceDrama.com

Made in the USA
Middletown, DE
12 March 2020